Praise for Alice

"[Oswald is] a perpetual in.
—James Wood, *The New Yorker*

"[Oswald's work] leaves me shaken and speechless."
—Edward Hirsch

"Oswald joins Ciaran Carson, Iain Sinclair, Hughes and
ultimately Joyce himself as one of the great celebrants
of the genius loci, the spirit of place, or what the Irish
call dinnseanchas, lovingly elaborated topographical
lore. . . . Oswald has soul in riverfuls."
—*Guardian*

"Alice Oswald is making a new kind of poetry. There is
nothing fancy about it—she is doing the job,
simple and enormous, of reworking the model for the
twenty-first century."
—Jeanette Winterson

"Alice Oswald's poems are vivid and distinct, alert and
deeply, physically engaged in the natural world."
—*Poetry Daily*

"Oswald's radiant poetry of remembrance
will not be readily forgotten."
—*Independent*

"A sublime poet of the natural world."
—*Herald*

"If there's any justice in the poetry world, the title [poet laureate] should be offered to this gardener-classicist who is bringing the British landscape to life in poetry again."
—*Daily Telegraph*

"You won't experience the full effect of Alice Oswald's poetry unless you read her words aloud—she writes with a mind for sounds, syllables, and the patters of speech, informed and inspired by oral storytelling traditions."
—*Bustle*

The Thing in the Gap-Stone Stile
Dart
Woods Etc.
The Thunder Mutters:
101 Poems for the Planet
(editor)
Weeds and Wild Flowers
Memorial
Falling Awake

A

SLEEPWALK

ON THE

SEVERN

ALICE OSWALD

W. W. NORTON & COMPANY

Independent Publishers Since 1923

NEW YORK | LONDON

Frontispiece: iStock.com/underworld111

For information about special discounts for bulk purchases, please contact
W. W. Norton Special Sales at specialsales@wwnorton.com or 800-233-4830

Manufacturing by Versa Press
Book design by JAM Design

Library of Congress Cataloging-in-Publication Data

Names: Oswald, Alice, 1966– author.
Title: A sleepwalk on the Severn / Alice Oswald.
Description: First American edition. | New York : W. W. Norton & Company, 2018. |
    Book-length poem.
Identifiers: LCCN 2018030535 | ISBN 9780393355970 (pbk.)
Subjects: LCSH: Moon—Poetry.
Classification: LCC PR6065.S98 S54 2018 | DDC 821/.914—dc23
LC record available at https://lccn.loc.gov/2018030535

W. W. Norton & Company, Inc., 500 Fifth Avenue, New York, N.Y. 10110
www.wwnorton.com

W. W. Norton & Company Ltd., 15 Carlisle Street, London W1D 3BS

1 2 3 4 5 6 7 8 9 0

A
SLEEPWALK
ON THE
SEVERN

This is not a play. This is a poem in several registers, set at night on the Severn Estuary. Its subject is moonrise, which happens five times in five different forms: new moon, half moon, full moon, no moon and moon reborn. Various characters, some living, some dead, all based on real people from the Severn catchment, talk towards the moment of moonrise and are changed by it. The poem, which was written for the Severn Project 2009, aims to record what happens when the moon moves over us—its effect on water and its effect on voices.

prologue

Flat stone sometimes lit sometimes not
One among many moodswung creatures
That have settled in this beautiful
Uncountry of an Estuary

Swans pitching your wings
In the reedy layby of a vacancy
Where the house of the sea
Can be set up quickly and taken down in an hour

All you flooded and stranded weeds whose workplace
Is both a barren mudsite and a speeded up garden
Full of lake offerings and slabs of light
Which then unwills itself listen

All you crabs in the dark alleys of the wall
All you mudswarms ranging up and down
I notice you are very alert and worn out
Skulking about and grabbing what you can

Listen this is not the ordinary surface river
This is not river at all this is something
Like a huge repeating mechanism
Banging and banging the jetty

.   .   .

Very hard to define, most close in kind
To the mighty angels of purgatory
Who come solar-powered into darkness
Using no other sails than their shining wings

Yes this is the moon this hurrying
Muscular unsolid unstillness
This endless wavering in whose engine
I too am living

NEW
MOON

Flooded fields by the Severn. Waveridge Sand,
only walked on by the Wind. Almost dark. New
Moon not yet risen. Car noise continuous.

Two sleepwalkers struggling along, one painfully
thin with eyes closed (that's the Moon), the other
writing, (that's me). I'm always out here, noting
things down in my nightbook being interrupted . . .

Enter a wobbling light. A bicycle. A Birdwatcher
with infra-red telescope. Off bicycle. Sets up tele-
scope and trains it on reeds. Gasps. Checks with
the naked eye. Makes bird calls. Shakes head.
Points telescope at reeds again. Shrieks.

birdwatcher   Impossible! Not here! Not now! Please not! Rare visitor. Rare? Not
breeding surely! Not now! Please!

Notice a fisherman walking home, with the Wind in rustling clothes
following.

fisherman   It's late. I don't like it walking on the mud at night.

A little horse trots through, knowing its way.

Did you see that?

Shhh!

Did you see that?

I'm so sorry. I'm going to have to ask you to be quiet. I'm recording all this in my nightbook.

(*whispering*)   I caught a really strange fish once, being about five foot in length and three foot in breadth, having two hands and feet and very grisly and wide-mouthed . . .

wind (*very emotional changeable*)   What happened please tell me
What happened to Florence Saunders

One minute a child next minute
A thousand years old
The wizened prisoner of the waters

Enter the satisfied sound of the river licking and sucking. There's the Fisherman with his foot stuck. The Birdwatcher 's watching. There's the Moon poor thing looking for eels among the reeds. She's asleep apparently. She's been walking since Dusk. She looks exhausted. Don't touch her. Keep moving the stones out of her way.

moon   Can't sleep. Little light left on. Low tide alongside me like a ploughed field. Nothing growing. Only the fresh cracked fat of the mud. Maybe seventeen or so white birds plop out across grey each whistling to itself and a hogweed seed whips over. Zzzipp. Can you see one. This is wetlands. Full of wildfowl. Keep looking. This is sediment. This is ordinary surface stuff with a shoe sticking out of the mud with a leg in it. Or is that a heron standing out of bounds on the reservoir Wall. which'll soon be twenty foot underwater

She begins to rise slowly through the trees and then out, shedding a weak, low buttery light, so that everything (even the stones) looks up:

chorus

Darklight darklight
It starts one night
With a little sleepless smallness.
A few stars creep out like cress

It starts at low tide
A tiny thing
The sun's unborn twin
Not wanting to be seen

A mere mouth
Not fully human
One side damaged, one side
Cringing to keep hidden

Is opening alone far down
Below mud-line
Still deeply snug in
Under the horizon

Aha!
There goes the little
White of her smile
Barely above dream-level

.   .   .

All mouth no face
Having no choice
But to be moon
Of all this space

She begins to climb
In her slimy death sheath
Very strong-willed and tugging
Tied to the earth

Enter a dreamer
Eyes closed. aghast
Sore feet
Having walked the road since dusk

Very hush hush
Very soft pedal
She begins to moan:
Is that all?

Not quite.
Night after night
The same night, I'm always
Trying to lift my body off its hook

.   .   .

But it's like searchlights out here
I keep being followed by a strip of light
I keep seeing the moon
Mother of all grasses

Maker of shadows snowface
Filling the paths of my gazes.
That's all
Goodnight

HALF

MOON

Three nights later, the night of the Half Moon. Muddy path by the
Severn. Mind your feet. Ninety-mile-an-hour wind across sand with
machine marks of hard-worked water. Two sleepwalkers struggling
along, one with eyes closed (that's the Moon not yet risen), the other
writing. Keep going. It's an estuary you see. And when the wind /
blows up you can be walking like this leaning forwards and you'll
still be going backwards . . .

Enter a bicycle. A Birdwatcher with infra-red telescope. Off bicycle.
Sets up telescope. Trains it on reeds. Sighs. Checks with the naked
eye. Makes bird calls. Shakes head. Returns to telescope. Swears.

birdwatcher   No long-billed dotterel!

Watches sharp, sea-wittled, mud-bred birds quite spaced out,
walking away along the tide-line. BANG! Enter Articled Clerk
with a gun.

articled clerk   Miserable weather. Bitterly bitterly cold.

Go away.

No feeling in my fingers.

Please. This is a nature reserve.

Excuse me, I need to retrieve my duck.

*Goose. Lesser white-fronted. We get about one a year round here
and you shot it.*

Duck actually.

*Goose infact. Silly fool. Notice a small tide creeping over the sand
quietly. Quite a drop here. Clay cliffs over reeds getting deeper.
Articled Clerk wades out. Wades out. Whooshing the bird towards
him. Reaches around, walking up to his waist and swims, struggles,
makes a grab for the bird and turns towards shore. Blue lips
trembling. Shouts 'Duck actually!' and disappears in the waves.
It's dawnless. Freezing cold hands, I can hardly write, no light. It's
gloom and offish water. Notice the Wind, very troubled, wading
through reeds.*

wind   Whisper whisper . . . this is
(restless   Harry Kingscott from Gloucester
neurotic)

              They found my cycle at the Wainlodes
              And my clothes not far off
              Please tell my mother they were folded

Enter a shriek. And another shriek, shaped like a curlew.

Please tell my mates
I saw the unseen shiny of one eye.
Glinting in its hood
And the other missing
I saw the Moon
Wandering asleep along the mudflats

Beginning to sway. Beginning to see things. I'm asleep apparently.
Keep going. This is quicksand. There's the Moon poor thing with
her foot stuck trying to lift.

moon   I'm asleep I think. Either that or dead. There's that light again.
What a drink it is. What a little dish of milk to be offered
to someone waking in the dark drinkless. Am I naked. My
stomach's full of gas. I can't remember what I'm looking for but
I've found shoes and skirts and ribbons here. And old crab lines
and fossils being wintered away and of course hundreds of half
fish half human mollusks and marine worms doubled up in
their undoing being slowly slipped out of the mud and made fat
again. It's exhausting. You can eat them but. I'm getting huge.
I'm getting stuck. Like a ship tipped over on its side called *The*
Resolute Lady

Up! She extricates her foot and begins to rise. Here's the sea coming
in. The Moon in curled-up form half-lit tipped slightly backwards
getting higher. Notice everything noticing:

chorus

This night is half moon night, half liquid every roof
This night a half out snail half feels the moonbraile
And things half seen wax and wane in the wind
Their leaves grow sharp and almost blue then blind

This night I'm half resigned the grasses only half sleep
This night is half moon night when the moon has
No feeling in her right side but she makes light of it
The cars dip their beams the wet fields have headlights

This night de-mists the dreamworld
This night is born the half strength shadow
Still pooling under my feet still half transfused
It's like I blot the world like on wet paper

This night it's lovely to stroll out
On a moon-walk sleepwatching on your feet
I'm going to stare up half this night
And then proceed by dreamsight, moonstinct

This night with eyes half closed
It's not so much what you see as what you are seeped in
And half next day the half sensation
Of many moon-shocked nerves half lit

FULL

MOON

This is several nights later. A lonely place where the Severn runs along lawns and lights that speak ship language in bright colours float past. There's the Wind on your ears like a hood. Two sleepwalkers struggling along, one huge with eyes closed, the other staring (that's me) being followed by a cloud. Keep going . . .

Enter a wobbling light. A bicycle. A Birdwatcher with infra-red telescope. Off bicycle. Sets up telescope. Points it at the water. Chuckles with joy. Checks with the naked eye. Consults book. Nods. Back to telescope. Looks through wrong end.

birdwatcher   The little stint! Or is it?

Turns telescope round. Looks through right end.

Not so little.

Enter immense sailor, spitting, coughing, roaring.
Oh for God's sake!

sailor   I need help! I need oxygen!

Grabs Birdwatcher by the throat as if to take his oxygen, thinks better of it, bursts into tears.
Could I help at all?

It's my heart. It's not working properly.

Aha. Birdwatcher grunts. Ungrunts. Snaps telescope shut. Waits for silence. Sailor shouts out endearments and curses as if looking for someone. Notice the wind sighing in the background, it keeps blowing the pages.

wind (*very*
downhearted
desperate)

Poor reeds
Standing in a draft in their night clothes

Sailor looks at the Moon. Looks at his hands. On his arm a heart with initials A.P. R.P. And underneath, an anchor.

Miserable weather
Wrinkled and tarnished water
Which smells of its fields

Sailor kisses the Moon. Poor thing. She enters her cloud. This is strange. Frozen fog look of the air. Dead hands of trees stroking the sky's fur.

There are stars, slowly coming closer with their torches. Notice something more than mere evening. Notice the white skirt of the Full Moon just under a cloud's edge. Beginning to wobble, jostling the reeds. She's asleep I think.

.   .   .

Notice flute music.

Notice a barn owl. Notice a feather bed being rowed across the river full of children. Notice flute music with children's voices and distant singing of the wind:

wind   Enter being dreamed
        Seven boats all sailed by blindmen
        Using flute music to determine the wind

        Somehow they feel their way seaward by the tune
        And exit

Enter the Moon.

moon   Looking round I remember who I am. This is water to one side
        of me. Eels etc. Little fires along the banks of the river and
        a few tins of cider in grasses. There's the owl. There's that
        horrible sucking sound. The glug glug of the tide. And it
        looks like a fairground the way the mud spreads out all lit
        up with a fisherman asleep walking over it. Checking his
        traps perhaps. Has he seen me. Halfway across. Tired out by
        dreams. He lets his feet sink in. He folds himself half shut
        with his legs gone dead and his coat still awake. Which feels
        like a window curtain blowing at night in a seldom entered
        room and in one of its folds there's a butterfly roosting

She begins to rise, shedding a black and white television screen light which picks out loneliness. Notice the Wind hasn't noticed. But the trees speak out with shadows in their voices:

chorus

Good God!
What did I dream last night?
I dreamt I was the Moon
I woke and found myself still asleep

It was like this: my face misted up from inside
And I came and went at will through a little peephole
I had no voice no mouth nothing to express my trouble
Except my shadows leaning downhill not quite parallel

Something needs to be said to describe my moonlight
Almost frost but softer almost ash but wholer
Made almost of water which has strictly speaking
No feature but a kind of counterlight call it insight

Like in woods when they jostle their hooded shapes
Their heads congealed together having murdered each other
There are moon-beings sound-beings such as deer and half deer
Passing through there whose eyes can pierce through things

I was like that: visible invisible visible invisible
There's no material as variable as moonlight
I was huge, trying to hide my moonhood, thinking
Good God! What did I dream last night?

NO
MOON

End of the month. Newnham-on-Severn. Very dark very wet. At
the end of Passage Lane where the ferry used to start. The Wind
lying wizened and crumpled on the water and a row of wooden
fence posts like the river's rotten teeth with a coat left hanging on
one.

Two sleepwalkers struggling along, one invisible with eyes closed,
the other writing. That's me. I'm always out here. Moving over
the night-map with the Moon my close friend following. A kind of
dream-secretary, always recording myself being interrupted, trying
to wake myself by writing. I'm doing well. Keep going. It's raining.
There's the birdwatcher already hidden in position, swaying with the
reeds with infra-red telescope. And here comes a Vicar on horseback
having trouble with his nose. Keeps covering the left nostril and
breathing in deeply and out. He can't keep his horse still.

vicar   Heavenly Father etc. On my way to Arlingham over the river.
Already late, Lord. No boat. Pretty angry now on account of

Enter to the right a married couple being washed downriver on a
sofa.

birdwatcher   Did you see that?

vicar   On account of the wind. Forgive me, Father. The rain I'm ok with
it's the ruddy wind that bothers me. It really stifles me. That's
why I would normally go by boat, Heavenly Father.

He sets out across the water on horseback, huffing his nose. Enter a
Parish Clerk, rowing to church with the register, shouting:

parish clerk   Almost all the cider both new and old's been damaged, the
                 hoarded apples carried away, the clean wheat in the bags
                 wetted, the cheese in the lofts and the butter in the dairy
                 hurted and the corn and hayricks up to the eaves in water, the
                 barns and threshing floors cleanly washed . . .

vicar   Damn!

The river's coming down rushed and troubled as if it's hiding
something. Enter Florence Saunders paddling. Harry Kingscott and
William George Montague, both with no shoes. Sarah Matthews,
epileptic, shouting curses at her mother. And the entire Bedford
family arguing. Enter unnamed sailor weeping with Matthias
Sydamnasta of Finland, holding a rung of rigging. William Cooper,
age 85, feverish, walking away fast with a bundle, grumbling. Enter
a small tide creeping over the sand quickly and several dogs howling
and in great distress. Enter eight people with ribbons coming back
from the fete. Paul Sweetland, staring at his hands. Thomas Knight
and Thomas Rooke in high spirits. James Knapp whistling.

Charles Fox, indignant with bruise marks. Two Westbury boys
holding their breath and Henry Bowyer still dry. Percy Simmonds,
Robert Nibblett, Jack Dudfield, Alex Bullock, Malcolm Hart. All

covered in mud, astonished. As well as Minnie Hyde and Ethel
Matthews And lastly, the Reverend John Lloyd Crawley's horse
with no rider, making its own way home.

birdwatcher   Has something happened? There's a hatstand here. There are
tables in the bushes and hundreds of wayfaring birds coming
down at angles to their mirrors. I could list all their names but
it's this coat that interests me . . .

wind   In the beginning people didn't die
(inconsolable)   They waxed and waned and
Here lie the very thin remains
Of a man

Sigh

Enter almost nothing
No more than the rim of an ear
Or the white of an eye

Over the fields, through the cold fingers of reeds, enter the Moon
almost gone, one last frost-crippled leaf left hanging on her
neckbone

moon   I'm getting older now. Lonely little marshlight moon. The wind's
blowing in my mouth bottle and it bags my cheeks out. Hold

tight. Extreme caution. I'll fall over I think. I'll let my legs crash on one side and sleep like old horsebones on a hill. It's damp but it's OK. I've done well. Have an eel. Lie here and let the wind sniff me over. Booing and bothering in my ears it's only the old wind again. He lives here. All those swearwords coming out of the air. There goes my light. Everything belongs to the wind now even these hands I don't care. I'm going to fall here. I'm going to curl up by the river all night and be slowly eroded by the wind. Fold up my clothes by the shore and sleep this grey crepuscular sleep that covers everything. It comes off on your fingers . . .

Enter absolute Darkness, full of the voice of the Wind:

wind (glum and with monotonous flute music)

The moon the moon comes up blind
Goes over to the trees looks out
Trying to find herself on a moonless night.
Puts her mind to the dark: where might I be found?

Where might an old woman in black
Slipping out at nightfall in the rain as far as the corner
Making her way by feel on the premiss of each footfall
Where might she be found?

She goes on and on asking
Groping for the threshold of sight
She creeps and leans on her cane till she can just make out
A dark place next door to a dark place

Puts her ear to her heart – no sound:
Where might I emerge in the midst of being rained away?
Steps on the fields without feet floats without face
Grumbling along under windows' insides out

She scans the surroundings by ultrasound
She finds windbones upside down
And the whoosh whoosh whoosh
Of a birdwing but no moon

    .   .   .

She finds hundreds of washed up sticks
And dead fish smells
And backings and forthings
Of water borrowing her being but no moon

She puts out her hands
Nothing
One or two stars but no moon
This is no good

She gives up
Soft little sigh with no mouth
Yes
This is not I

MOON

REBORN

Flooded fields by the Severn. Waveridge Sand, only walked on by the Wind. Almost dark, waiting for the Moon to be reborn. Car noise continuous. Two sleepwalkers struggling along, one small, barely there, with eyes closed, the other writing . . .

Enter a wobbling light. A bicycle. A Birdwatcher with infra-red telescope. Off bicycle. Sets up telescope and trains it on reeds. Gasps. Checks with the naked eye. Makes bird calls. Shakes head. Points telescope at reeds again. Shrieks.

birdwatcher Impossible! Not here! Not now! Please not! Not breeding surely! Not now! Please!

Notice a fisherman walking home.

fisherman It's late. I don't like it walking on the mud at night.

birdwatcher Have you seen this?

fisherman That's a most peculiar fish.

A little horse trots through, knowing its way.

Did you see that?

birdwatcher Shhhh!

fisherman	What is it? What have you seen?
birdwatcher	Thirty turnstones. One bar-tailed godwit. One Bewick swan. So far.
fisherman	I saw a woman here last week. Very strange. From the County Prison I should think. Most probably epileptic. And just now a horse.
birdwatcher	I'm so sorry. I'm going to have to ask you to be quiet. I'm waiting for something quite rare.
fisherman (*whispering*)	I caught a really strange fish once, being about eight foot tall and completely circular very peaceful and wide-eyed with wings . . .
wind (*very excitable with flute*)	Another thousand years The Moon, mother of many rivers Has grown young again

It could happen to anyone
Whose being both dims and widens
As if carried by the wind

*It's Dusk. There's the barn owl. There's the Moon poor thing in
human form rising slowly through the trees and then out, shedding
a razor-sharp wince of light. And this is me, the Dream Secretary,
recording all this at moonrise, 31st of the 8th and hereafter. Notice
the water rising. Notice everyone all up and down the valley looking
up and singing:*

birdwatcher

The Birdwatcher moves quietly,
Seeing his way in the dark.

White-throated, splay-footed,
Sways with the reeds,
Watching the swans in their kitchens.

All night the piercing police whistle curlews
Are searching the marshes,
Keeping the river on red alert, but he kneels
Non-descript in his hide,
From headland to headland
His blue eyes glide not blinking.

He sees everything:
The grebe's nest under the weed,
The waders resting on fold-up stools along the tideline.

Everything down to the lowest least whisper
Of ducks tucked in self-pillow
And meals wriggling under stones,

Even the shiver of an owl's wing
Moving through stars

        he perfectly hears . . .

  .   .   .

At last at low water he stands up,
Remembering his heavy feet.

Now he splashes away through the heavenly reed fields
And the numberless pools of the Dawn . . .
Behind his back there are twenty tiny goddesses
Washing their dresses in the waves.

And the doves in the woods
Clap awake when he walks.

fisherman

Another thousand years,
The moon, mother of many rivers,
Has grown young again.
It could happen to anyone
Whose being both dims and widens
As if carried by the wind.

A man for example,
Sitting very still in his bone-web,
Dipped in old age up to the eyes,
When the tide recedes, his arms
Draggle to his sides
As hollow as reeds.

Another thousand years,
Every twelve hours,
Every vein in the valley re-fills its syringe
At the thought of the moon:
The marsh grass prickles its hackles
And the trees speak out with shadows in their voices.

And a man for example,
Sitting very still in his bone-web,
Dipped in old age up to the eyes,
When the tide returns he runs
Thigh-deep through the Severn,
Chasing the lightning of a salmon.

articled clerk

This evening those very thin fence posts
Struggled up out of the mud again
And immediately the meal began, there was
That flutter of white napkins of waders hurrying in

There was that bent old egret
Prodding and poising his knife and fork
And so many mucous mudglands
So much soft throat sucking at my feet

I thought be careful this is deep mud this is
Pure mouth it has such lip muscles
Such a suction of wet kisses
The slightest contact clingfilms your hands

There goes that dunlin up to her chin in
The simmering dish of mush and
All night that seeping feeding sound
Of moistness digesting smallness

And then I creep-slid out over the grey weed
And all those slimy food pods burst under me
I thought I know whose tongue I'm
Treading on and under whose closed eye

.   .   .

Every shoe every shell every sock
Every bone will be crammed in.
To my unease the meal went on and on
There were those queues of reeds

Dipping their straws in the dead
There was that sly tide swiftly refilling.
I thought really I should have webbed feet
I should have white wings to walk here

crowds lining the banks

It's incredible when she visits her rivers,
Dragging her wave like a ghost-robe
Right across the sea and earth and through everything

And everyone jumps into cars and starts driving
Urgently towards her, hypnotised together by the greylight
And they stand on the bank, zipped up, staring through cameras,
Or pressed into pub windows, or under the willows in the rain,
Running through fields in wetsuits, whooping,
Wanting to ride the very rim of the river-wheel
To be rolled bodily along in its drowning,
It's incredible when she lights the touch-paper of her power

Sometimes she seems to have swum here
Leaving a trail of moon-slime on the line of the current

But it's incredible when she moves blind as a mole, groping her way
    forwards
And the smoky shine of water in its worn-out shoes
Goes slower and slower and slower till the whole valley
Glimmers and glimmers like the Summer of the Underworld

And sometimes at the very moment of her passing,
Which is like a riverquake, like the weight of the sea,
Like the interstellar cold coming suddenly into the world,
A man nips into the loo and misses the whole thing,

And when he comes out, there's everyone clapping and hooting
And the river rushing backwards trying to retrieve itself,
It's as if he'd waited two thousand years for a comet
Which came when his back was turned, it's incredible

It's incredible when she chooses to push
The river right over without caring,
And there's the earth dangling in emptiness
With its feet kicking the air, it's incredible
When she floats along in her havoc not breathless at all

mother

I'm waiting for a Barn Owl.
Keeping my patience intact
For a whiter, much quieter creature
Made of kite-struts and knife-blades.

Waiting for a power
Appearing only when the fog is in flower
And the spiders close off all routes into the fields.

With the fingers of dusk unbending slowly,
Coming slowly, more painfully alive.

(Out of reach! Out of reach!
She will work her shift
Like a mechanic expertly unboning a car without speaking,

Pulling the cords of her wings
Like two stiff sails . . .)

I'm waiting for an old frayed queen
To walk to that window:

She who shines like the Moon,
But shits on the walls,
She whose house has no books in it
Or bath.

.   .   .

She who stares at her dead child
And never tidies away
Its rat-eaten cradle clothes . . .

Waiting for whatever hard-worked mother
Owns those feathery bones.

Some kind of lightning unlikeness
To teach me her meekness.

epileptic

Every night I walk this way
The moony river paths,
Watching with a growing eye
The riffs and rags of moths.

Oh gentle moths that follow me,
I'll let you hear my mind
Concerning things that brush up close
And vanish like the wind.

Every night the sea runs in
Over a slum of sand.
It takes all week to watch the tide
And several years to know the wind.

I put my foot down on the grass,
I thought it was a path,
But first it sighed and then it sank.
I wish I was a white-winged moth.

I wish I was that whirring flutter
Way out over the shaking reeds.
Between the breezes and myself
Hard to say which would be lighter.

vicar

Sometimes you see mudfish
Those short lead lengths of eels
That hide at low tide
Those roping and wagging
Preliminary pre-world creatures, cousins of the moon
Who love blackness aloofness
Always move under cover of the unmoon
And then as soon as you see them
                gone
Untranslatable hissed interruptions
Unspeakable wide chapped lips
It's the wind again
Cursing the water and when it clears

You keep looking and looking for those
Underlurkers, uncontrolled little eddies
When you lever their rooves up
They lie limbless hairless
Like the bends of some huge plumbing system
Sucking and sucking the marshes and
Sometimes it's just a smirk of ripples
And then as soon as you see them
                gone
Untranslatable hissed interruptions
Unspeakable wide chapped lips
It's the wind again
Bothering the reeds and when it clears

.   .   .

You keep looking and looking for those
Backlashes waterwicks
You keep finding those sea-veins still
Flowing, little cables of shadow, vanishing
Dream-lines long roots of the penumbra
But they just drill down into gravel and
Dwindle as quick as drips
And then as soon as you see them
                    gone
Untranslatable hissed interruptions
Unspeakable wide chapped lips
It's the wind again
Pushing on your ears and when it clears

Sometimes you see the whip-thin
Tail of a waning moon start
Burrowing back into blackness
And then as soon as you see her
And then as soon as you say so
                    gone

dream secretary

Last thing each night, go out for the moon.
Pull on old coat, shut garden gate.
Roll up old sleeves. Swing arms. Poor soul.
Think moonset. Moonrise. All running to schedule.
World black and white. Walk up the lane.
Last thing each night. Look up for the moon.
No sign but rain. Almost back home.
One more last quick. Glance up for the moon.

Eyes stripped to the darkness. Can't help but notice
Little desklamp glow. As from upstairs window.
Shoulder of a woman. There, that's her.
Very old poor soul, maybe all but gone.
Last thing each night, flick on flick off.
Flick on flick off. Little hand torch halo.
There that's her. Last thing each night,
Letting only the light of a white sleeve show.

Sometimes the moon is more an upstairs window,
Curtains not quite drawn but lit within and lived in.
And sometimes the moon is less and
Sometimes she moves behind and sometimes she's gone.
Sometimes it's the moon. Sometimes it's the rain.

ACKNOWLEDGEMENTS

I'm very grateful to the following for their contributions to the poem: Joe Ray, Karen Cooke, Percy Heywood, Jonathon Crump, James Greenwood, Chris Witts, Sue Dubois, Michael Jeffries, Colin Kavanagh, Peter Wisschussen and the crew of the Sara Lifeboat. Also to Peter Oswald, Charles Boyle, Paul Keegan, Jo Bousfield, Helen Owen, Laura Beatty and all the Keens and all members of Taurus Voice: Elle Holiday, Penelope Rubach, Adrian Locher, Adrian Brett and Philippa Williams Brett. Thanks also to Richard Headon and John Beddell from Desperate Men, and to Sean Borodale, some of whose ideas (from 'The Salthouse Field Survey') I've borrowed. Also to Gloucestershire County Council for commissioning this work.

ABOUT THE AUTHOR

Alice Oswald lives in Devon and is married with three children. *Dart*, her second collection, won the T. S. Eliot Prize in 2002. Her third collection, *Woods etc*, is a Poetry Book Society Choice and was shortlisted for the Forward Prize for Best Collection and the T. S. Eliot Prize. *Falling Awake*, her most recent collection, won the Costa Poetry Award and the Griffin Poetry Prize.